T0171449

Stepping Out of Line

Have Both Feet In Or Two Feet Out

C.C. Rose

WestBow
PRESS
A DIVISION OF THOMAS NELSON

Copyright © 2013 C.C. Rose.

All rights reserved. No part of this book may be used or reproduced by any means, graphic, electronic, or mechanical, including photocopying, recording, taping or by any information storage retrieval system without the written permission of the publisher except in the case of brief quotations embodied in critical articles and reviews.

WestBow Press books may be ordered through booksellers or by contacting:

WestBow Press
A Division of Thomas Nelson
1663 Liberty Drive
Bloomington, IN 47403
www.westbowpress.com
1-(866) 928-1240

Because of the dynamic nature of the Internet, any web addresses or links contained in this book may have changed since publication and may no longer be valid. The views expressed in this work are solely those of the author and do not necessarily reflect the views of the publisher, and the publisher hereby disclaims any responsibility for them.

Any people depicted in stock imagery provided by Thinkstock are models, and such images are being used for illustrative purposes only.

Certain stock imagery © Thinkstock.

ISBN: 978-1-4497-7910-8 (sc)
ISBN: 978-1-4497-7909-2 (e)

Library of Congress Control Number: 2012923499

Printed in the United States of America

WestBow Press rev. date: 1/2/2013

I was deceived because of how it was perceived
Was blind, but now I see
Greek life versus God's life for me
Slaving to climb the same step over and over again
Conforming to somebody's image
Allowing the Holy Spirit to work through me
Changing lives one page at a time.

Table of Contents

Preface

Everything in life is black and white. Either it is one way or the other. Deception creates the idea of there being a grey area; where the thought of living on both sides (God and Satan) is ok and excusable. It is not. Many have fallen into this trap but seldom do people get out because of the lack of knowledge. I am one of those seldom people that got delivered from the grey area of deception. In this case, the deception was that sororities and fraternities are Christian based organizations doing the things of God, which is far from the truth.

There is a saying that says actions speak louder than words. In this case, the actions and words of the Greek Lettered Organizations are speaking equally as loud and clear about their mission and place in secret societies. *Stepping out of Line*, is a book that will give insight on the truth about Greek Lettered Organizations (both Divine 9 and the rest) and what God says about them. I am writing this book from my perspective, directed by the Holy Spirit. I will take you through my story from past (Part I) to present (Part II). As a right to privacy, I will not disclose the names of individuals, the sorority I was a part of, nor the university I attended.

The purpose of writing, *Stepping Out of Line* is so that everyone has access to a different perspective on Greek Life. Often times, the story of Greek Life is told from the perspective of a current member of a Greek Lettered Organization. However, *Stepping Out of Line* brings a new perspective on the subject of whether or not Christians should be a part of a sorority or fraternity. I want to make sure that you as the reader understand that it is not my position to tell anyone whether or not they should join or leave a Greek Lettered Organization. However, it is my responsibility to shed knowledge on a topic that many people want answers to. I hope my testimony blesses you and confirms your position on the issue one way or the other.

Last but certainly not least, I would like to thank my mom, dad, sister, family and close friends for being the support I need as I continue to spread the Lord's Gospel. I want to thank my first love, who is my Savior, Jesus Christ for everything. I am thankful and grateful to have the opportunity to serve in your Name and advance Your Kingdom for Your glory.

Part I: My Story

Chapter 1:
Why I joined a Sorority

There are three main reasons why I joined a sorority: I wanted to be a part of something that was larger than myself, I wanted to create a close knit family bond since I was away from home, and lastly through these avenues aforementioned, I was attempting to discover myself away from the influences of my comfort zone (family, friends, etc..). As a naive college freshmen fresh from the over protection of my parent's home, I started my journey in a place where for four years I would call home. I graduated high school from a small town where everyone knew each other, where no one was a stranger. Arriving at the university, I wanted to mimic this close knit family atmosphere into my new life journey and education.

Before I stepped foot on campus, I was very clear that I did not want to join a sorority. I thought it was very odd and conforming how everyone looked exactly the same, and how complete strangers now called each other sisters and yet they may not have known one another for even three weeks. I did not want to lose my individuality and what made me unique. Loss of individuality was what I saw on the surface when I witnessed sorority girls around campus. So, you might be asking how I went from initially not ever wanting to join a sorority to becoming a member of one. Great question, and now I will explain how it happened.

My first semester at college was pretty standard. My routine was pretty much class, student union, dorm room, sleep, class, student union, dorm room, sleep, etc. This routine that I had was very comforting to me and I was completely fine with it. I had my best friend from high school rooming with me in the dorms so there was no need in my mind, to do much else outside of my daily routine. Except there was one problem, I was still feeling the void of not having a close knit group that I could be a part of and at the time I did not find a church home to be a part of that was the right fit for me. I wanted to be a part of something larger than myself so that I felt like what I was doing mattered and made a difference in the lives of others.

With this void still needing to be filled, second semester of freshmen year I began to seek options and opportunities. I started to write poetry for the African American Student Affairs Newsletter, started meeting more people and lifetime friends, and I even joined a Collegiate Scholars program. But somehow it still wasn't enough to satisfy what I was looking for. So, I started to look at the one area I said I would never ever go in to: Greek life. Greek Life at the college I attended was very present and active. At the time, it seemed as if over 45% of students that attended were a part of a Greek Lettered Organization (GLO). So, the option of joining a sorority seemed likely since that was in the forefront most of the time.

As I began to take a closer look at Greek life, I found that what I was looking for in terms of finding my place could be found in these GLO's. I wanted a home away from home, people who I could depend on, a "family," people who I could trust and always be around knowing that we were there for each other. Now, most of the Greek organizations fit this criteria and it was up to me to dig deeper and find out exactly which one was the best fit for me.

I looked at all of the Greek Councils and did research on specific sororities and still did not find one that was best fitting for me. It wasn't until perhaps a few weeks later when a particular sorority hosted an informational meeting that I realized I might have found the right fit for me. This sorority was not listed in any of the pamphlets or brochures that were sent out so it seemed as if this sorority popped up out of thin air. So, I went ahead and proceeded to find out more about it.

At the informational, the members were very impressive. They were very informing and were quick to assure us as the listeners that they were loving, about sisterhood and family, community service and education. They emphasized that it was a lifetime commitment and that it does not stop at the end of college like some traditional Greek Organizations. This all sounded very well and my interest was very keen at that point.

One of the main highlights of the informational meeting was finding out that this particular sorority was about family, inclusiveness and love. This was of particular interest to me because it truly made me feel like the members were truly about relationships, bonding and being able to provide and be there for one another for a common goal. That was exactly what I was looking for; a group of people who shared the same interests as me, loved education and were going through the same issue I was which was establishing a home away from home.

Once I took the time to think, pray, and speak to family and the people who were going to endure the initiation process with me, I then decided to make my own decision to make a lifetime commitment to the organization. Once I informed the organization of my decision I had no idea of how much my life was going to change. And now the process of becoming a new member begins.

Chapter 2:
The Process

The initiation process for going through a predominately African American Greek organization is unique and in many respects frightening. In this chapter, I am going to take you through the mindset I was in, how I felt and the compromises I made as a result of the initiation process. The purpose of the initiation process is to break an individual down and build them up as one with their line into the organization. Now, their history becomes the organization's history with a new name, new walk, and new life. To begin, most things are done in secret. If a person is not of the organization, there are simply certain things one will never know. This information is protected by fear and pride of its members.

The Paperwork

In the beginning of the initiation process things seemed fairly mild. After the informational, and establishing that you want to be a part of that particular organization, they ask you once again, "are you sure you want to join this sorority? It is a lifetime commitment". Once you say yes to them, let the mind games begin. The first step in my process was to have another meeting with the members of the chapter as well as the other young ladies that I was going through the process with. Of course there was a period before this meeting where we had to complete other necessary requirements such as community service and maintaining a certain Grade Point Average.

For the meeting, I dressed in a nice pink blouse and black slacks. My first mistake was wearing pink to the meeting. The sorority's colors were not pink, so to them it was almost offensive that I would even come into their presence with anything other than the traditional black and white, or the sorority colors. But even then, it was a Catch 22 because if I had worn the sorority colors to please them, it would have been just as bad as wearing another sorority's colors.

Ok, back to the "paper work" of the business meeting. At this meeting, the other young ladies and I were told multiple times that this was a non-hazing organization and that they do not tolerate any physical or verbal abuse being placed on the new initiates. This was the first lie. Then, we read out loud a few pages about what entailed of the organization and what was to be expected of the process. I do not remember too many details on the paper, however I do remember the process and remembering it was nothing like what was said in this meeting. After we signed the paperwork and officially agreeing to become a member of the sorority, next up was an interview. In this interview, there was a panel of about five or six members who held high positions on the both the local, state and regional boards. In this meeting, each of us was pulled inside of a room individually for a one on one interview. The interview was similar to a job interview so no questions were out of the ordinary.

After the interview, we waited for the paperwork to process on the national level, and then the mental and physical aspect of the initiation process began.

Blindfolded with Fear

The first day, my line sisters and I get a call that we are to be ready by a certain hour because some of the sorority members were going to pick us up. We were told ahead of time to wear all white and we all had to match and essentially look the same in every way, nothing could be individual about us. We did not know where we were going, who was going to be there or what was going to happen but one thing we did know was inquiring about those questions was not an option. About half way to our destination, which was very far, they stopped in the middle of nowhere at a gas station. They then told us to get out of the car, and that point the proceeded to blindfold us. This was the first red flag. The lesson that was immediately put into place was along this process all that we had were each other because who knows what was to come.

After they blindfolded us, we got back into the car and drove to the destination, of which we did not know. Once we arrived, we were guided to a room where our blindfolds were taken off. There we were in a room with other girls whom we gathered were from another university. The members of the sorority gave us a multiple choice test and we were instructed to take the exam. We were not to talk or look around the room.

The test consisted of questions about the history of the organization and its affiliates. After we took the test we were immediately blindfolded again and lead outside and into the car. They drove us around and began to tell us that we got most of the answers wrong. Mind you, we were not taught this information because we were expected to know it already. Now, before we met up with them, my line sisters at the time, and I did some research ahead on the organization so that we could be prepared. Our preparation did not help. For some of those answers I know we got right but they said we got it wrong. They never told us the right answers nor did we ask what they were.

Ritual 1: Say What?

When we got back to the house the same day, still blindfolded we were guided back to an area outside. We had to wait for a while because they were still setting up. It was rather hot outside so they gave us an ice cube to eat while we waited. I wanted to say, can a "sister" get a few ice cubes in a glass of water? In no time, we were inside of the house. As we entered into the house, the members of the sorority were singing a hymn/chant of the sorority. We walked in blindfolded and holding hands. After we were all in and they finished singing the hymn, the president of the graduate chapter then told us to repeat after her the oaths to the organization.

Still to this day I could not tell you what I said, but I do remember sections of the oath being questionable and some parts disagreeable, but out of fear I said nothing and proceeded to take the oath. At this time, all initiate members are on their knees raising their right hand. Everyone including the initiates were wearing white. The entire set up of this ritual seemed weird and not normal. I was thinking why do I have to do all of this just to be a part of a sisterhood?

When the blindfolds were taken off, we were each given a candle. We then lit the candles and after that, unfortunately I do not remember. It is sad what fear can do to a person. After this, they said we were done and that was the end of ritual one. We then took pictures outside. Now in our minds, we didn't know if we were allowed to hold the sorority hand sign up or not. When the women of the sorority said the phrase "you guys are done" it was very unclear as to what that really meant.

Once we were done taking photos outside, we went into the kitchen area where there was food and beverages. To be honest my antennas were up and I did not want to eat anything. And moments later, the next phase of the night began.

The Break Down

That same night, when we thought we were in the clear and officially into the organization, here comes a twist to the happy ending. It all started when one of my lines sisters had to go to the restroom. When she was in the restroom, a sorority member started yelling at us saying that if one of us had to go to the restroom, then we all have to go to the restroom. I know, sounds crazy right? That's because it is. So we just got close to each other, and went by the door waiting for her to get out of the bathroom. Once she got out of the bathroom, we were told to line up side by side and link up. At this point the yelling and tests are coming in full force. One member walked behind us and others started saying, "oh so you're just going to have your backs to her?" Having our backs to a sorority member is a sign of disrespect so from that point on we were to say, "Excuse our backs ma'am." Speaking of ma'am, we had to address everyone in the organization as the sorority's name with ma'am added at the end.

One member tried to "break our line" or attach herself to the end or front of the line. The members were yelling at us telling us to do something to prevent her from breaking our line. Paralyzed in

11

fear, we just stood there. I believe one time we tried to do something but that idea was immediately shut down. The lesson was that we were not to let anyone break our line wherever we were. We were one and no one else outside of the organization can be added to it. We had to look out for each other no matter what. If someone had confrontation with one of us, someone had confrontation with all of us. This was the mentality that we had.

Another incident that happened on this day was with my belt. That night, I happened to have a belt on. Well, since no one else had a belt on that was not considered being "one," it was considered as me still wanting to be an individual. So, some of the members told us we all had to pretend we had on belts, so we all had to pretend (except me since I had on the belt) to take on and off the belt and put it in a bag. These were just some of the things that we had to endure during the initiation process that had us scared to even move, literally. I felt bad for the girls from the other university because it seemed they had it worse than we did. Now since I was the "ace" or first person in the line, I was responsible for everyone and everything. If there was something to be said, I was to say it and I was responsible for everyone knowing the information. I was "in charge" if you will.

At this point we were told to sit on the floor against the wall. We were then given more instructions and commands. It started with the bag that was given to us. In the bag, there was a small object, a small notebook and a pen. We could only write in blue or black ink. As you can see, everything is based on color. One's identity is in the color of the organization; hence the idea of conforming, being one and looking alike uniformly. With the small object, we were to make it look presentable. So no other colors except the sorority's colors were allowed to be on the small object. We all had to carry the small object EVERYWHERE we went. I mean everywhere, and if we were to run into one of the members and we did not have the small object, it would have been a price to pay.

It's a good thing we did not run into any of them on campus. The notebook was given to us so that when we met up at these "meetings" we were to write down everything they told us to and it had to be written EXACTLY the same in everyone's notebook. If it wasn't, they threatened to rip out the pages and we would have to start over. We would have to write things like, how to dress, how to keep ourselves maintained because we represented the organization so of course they didn't want us looking unprofessional or not "put together". We had to write down when the next Conference will be, also the names, line names and phone numbers of everyone in that room. It was a must that we remember each of their names too. As you can see, there was no room for mistake here in this process and organization. As a side note, we were given a temporary pin that we always had to wear no matter what, and the same went with the official pin once we officially became members of the sorority.

Singing Our Hearts Out!

There were parts of the process that after we crossed we could laugh at, but at the time it was not funny at all. For example, we had to come up with songs for our deans. (By the way, every time we had to come with something we had a night to do so). This typically is a traditional thing that is done. I don't know the exact reason for it but from what I gather is it is a song that displays the dean's character and how great of a person they are. During the times we had to sing them their song, I had no idea how to sing or harmonize but I think we did pretty good for a spur of the moment deal. There were "fun" moments that happened in the sorority but compared to my overall experience it doesn't compare.

Information Overload: Were we Supposed to Know That?

There were many times when we were in meetings where we were being yelled at by the sorority members, asking us for information we did not know and could not recite and the same time. Everything we did and said had to be done and recited at the same time. Our responses were to be together and if they weren't they wanted to know why. I tell you during these two weeks of my life, I felt nothing but fear, frustration, fatigue, and anger. I should've known these feelings were not going away after the initiation process was done. The sorority members were showing their true nature to us then but fear was in the way of any of us recognizing it.

There would be times where we wanted to give up and call it quits because it was just too much. I was tired of being yelled at and treated less than who I was because I didn't know everything there was to know about the organization as a whole including information about the chapter. There were so many dates, people and groups that had to be memorized, I felt like I had been given a history lesson but in the form of a test and failed it every time. It was as if I was going to school full time but yet building a chapter from scratch while being pressured in to cramming all the sorority's history into my brain. Can you say information overload! Anyone in their right mind would never go through this twice, ask anybody who is in a Black Greek Lettered Organization (BGLO).

It was very uneasy every day not knowing what was going to happen at one of these meetings. We didn't know who was going to be there or what was going to be told of us to do, think or say. Sometimes, these "meetings" lasted all night. Up until that point, my line sisters and I were working day and night and were expected to perform in excellence in all areas with no sleep. Outrageous.

Scholarship IS One of The Pillars Right?

Going through an initiation process takes up a lot of time both in the day and night. I am not exactly sure at what point in the process, perhaps somewhere in the middle, when things started to get pretty busy with this process and school. Not to mention we went through this process about a month out from finals. For anyone who knows me, I am very committed to my academics. No thing or person is going to get in my way of obtaining my education. Well, slowly but surely this initiation process was pulling me away from my studies and study time. I was not happy about this. I am not a person to always have something to say, but there are some exceptions to this and interfering with my education was one of them.

Not only did I need more time for my school work, so did my line sisters, and they had tougher courses than I did at the time. Believe it or not, I was actually scared to ask if we could have some time during these "meetings" for our homework. I spoke up anyway and wrote a letter to one of our deans and asked if we could bring our homework. We were allowed to, but it was not a pleasant process. The dean made us feel like asking her if we could bring our homework during one of these sessions was one of the most insane questions.

It is almost as if the dean didn't want us to do our homework. We were supposed to somehow make it work even though we were in class all day and with them all night. Red flag #2, I should have known, in their eyes nothing comes before the sorority even though they say otherwise. I had to think to myself, this organization does have a pillar of scholarship right? It didn't seem like it during the process and it didn't seem like it after. I started off my college career with a 4.0 GPA and by the time I finished my first full year in the org, I was in the 2.5 range. I was not happy. Not to mention, my stress level increased dramatically and never came down.

Ritual 2: Is it really Over?

As time passed, so did our individualities. By this time I was ready for the end of the initiation process to come. Every day it seemed as if that day wasn't going to come anytime soon. During ritual two, we were taken to a location. At this location, we were sent in a room along with some other ladies from the other university. It was at this time we made sure we knew all of the information that we learned in the past two weeks. It was time for some relief. We knew that it was the end but we were unsure of what would happen if we could not say the information correctly and simultaneously. When it was time for us to present our information, we were blindfolded and led downstairs as everyone else was singing the song, "In my heart, and my soul is the sorority." (Just writing this brings back some feelings and memories I wish not to revisit. But I will for the sake of encouraging others to stay out or get out of these organizations.) At this time we were still blindfolded.

If you have ever been blindfolded and had to trust the very people who were yelling at you and were your so called, "sisters", you would understand the fear that would creep up in one's mind. After we stopped walking and were in the room, we stood still. They then proceeded to tell us to from beginning to end say all that we knew about the organization. Just to give you an idea, this had to be done all in one voice, meaning everyone says everything at the same time, no stutters, mumbling or mistakes. I think I was more nervous in this part of the process than any of my line sisters were. I was nervous because I felt like if I didn't pass this then I did this entire process for nothing, or even worse, the process would last longer. At this point I just wanted out. As I will explain later I felt I was going further into the wrong direction. Sin will take a person farther than they ever wanted to go. This was just the beginning of this interesting path.

After we all went through our information and said it to their satisfaction, we were guided around a table still blindfolded. At this table they took the veil off of our eyes and said some last words. There we received our official pin, and had to blowout a lit candle as a significance of the end (I believe that was the reason). At this point everyone begins to celebrate. I was still in the mode of fear so I did not fully accept the fact that it was done until a good 30 minutes from that point. Of course, our titles changed. We went from being initiates to neophytes, which meant we were new and young to the organization. This also meant, we still had work to do. For example, after we celebrated, we had to clean the entire kitchen while most of the prophytes talked amongst themselves and with us. I never have been accustomed to being told what to do from people I hardly know. Needless to say the journey after the process begins with the big S word, STRESS.

Chapter 3:
Laboring in Vain

In this chapter I am going to speak about the two year journey that I experienced with this organization. There was a combination of highs and lows, pain and struggle, smiles and tears. This two year period is part of the result of my testimony. I will speak about the positives from being in this organization as well as the countless struggles that I faced. Being in a BGLO, everything we had was earned and we had to work very hard for it. We had to earn it to deserve it. Grace and mercy were two words that didn't show up very much or not at all. One of the key lessons I've learned from this experience is to always put God's Word first and never waiver or settle.

Presidency

After we had our probate, and were officially members of the organization, the stress and non-stop movement began. Prior to my line coming out, the sorority was not officially on campus. So, we had the pressure of going through the steps to re charter the chapter on campus and get it started from the ground, up. This entire process was one that strengthened me and really showed me what I can do and what I was capable of when dealing with unfavorable circumstances. The same month that we crossed over to the sorority, we had to decide who was going to be in what executive position so that we could prepare for the application process that was required through the university that I was attending. In that month, it was decided that I was going to be president of the chapter. You might ask did I not want to be president? The answer is no, I did not. However, the rest of the line didn't want to do it and encouraged me to fill the position, so that's what ended up happening.

All summer, it was preparation time for the fall and what was to come with meeting with the Fraternity and Sorority Programming (FSP). Keep in mind we did not have a probate, or coming out show, until three months after we crossed, so everything that we did no one could know about it. After the probate, in due time we became an official club/organization on campus. This was exciting news for us because now we had more resources and support from the school to advance and enhance the chapter. For me, this meant my organization skills had to be top notch because I had no idea the amount of work that was coming my way. My term as president was very interesting. In public, I loved it because it was part of the façade, but in private I didn't love it so much.

25% Equals 100%

The advice that I received from the graduate chapter president at the time was that in any given chapter 25% of the people are going to do the work and the rest do nothing. Well since there were only four of us it meant that unfortunately, I was the 25% and there was nothing that could be done to make the others participate more. These words were not very encouraging to me since I was stressed to the max.

This presidency was new and the fact that the graduate chapter was not in the same city as we were, I had no tangible example to look up to for consistent guidance and support. I knew that without the proper support from the members of the chapter that it was going to be an uphill battle.

I remember I had a conversation with the current president at the time from the graduate chapter and I expressed to her my frustrations; some of which came from not having the full cooperation of the other members in the chapter. It was understood and highly suggested that school and the sorority be the top priority. At the time it seemed to me that I was the only one that made that transition of making school and the sorority priority because the others were focused on other activities and clubs that they were a part of. I was crying, frustrated and in need of some answers. I tried everything to make it easy for the other members to participate and get their tasks done but nothing seemed to work.

It didn't help that the graduate chapter president said that it was just reality and unfortunately in any given chapter whether there are four in the chapter or 400, only 25% do the hard work of the sorority; the rest will be a face or put the sorority on the back burner. Although the image of what I thought the sorority life was going to be like began quickly diminishing, I kept moving through one long storm that never ended.

The Labor

At this point in my story, I want to take you through some of the general day to day activities and organizing that I had to do in my role as president. Later in the chapter I will give more detailed examples. One of the things that was for certain was there were always a handful of meetings each month. Between the chapter meetings, sorority state meetings, President's meetings held by FSP, FSP meetings with the NPHC advisor, NPHC meetings, and conference calls over the phone, I felt like a business woman with school as a part time job. Not to mention my grades reflected how much time I was investing in the sorority and not my education, and the results were not to my satisfaction. During this time, I was also a peer mentor for a freshmen retention program at the university I attended which meant I taught once a week and held individual meetings with my students every week. So as you can see I was pretty busy during the semester.

For the sorority meetings, I was in charge of creating the agenda and preparing the topics and time limits of each. I also was charged with the duty of conducting the meetings and when I was absent, I made a list of the items to go over and the time limit so that it was a smooth meeting. During these meetings we talked about the progress, or lack thereof on certain issues, updates, resources, and plans for the future of the chapter, especially expansion towards the middle and end of my term. These meetings were usually held on Saturday mornings and lasted for 2 hours in the morning. We all had busy school and work schedules so when we did have a day off on Saturday, we spent the morning in meetings. It had to be this way to get things accomplished, but it still contributed to the very busy schedule of all members.

You would think a two hour meeting would be productive right? Wrong. Most of these meetings seemed to go nowhere and only accomplish 25% of the things on the agenda and list of things that needed to be done. Needless to say the meetings were not as efficient as they could have been; too many opinions and less agreement on issues. Might I mention that there was more work for us because we were re-chartering the chapter on campus so we had to work at the 200% level instead of the normal 100%.

Another way that our chapter communicated was through meetings over the phone. Since I was the president, I was the voice and representation of the chapter, so this meant that I had to listen in and attend all of these meetings. Mind you, since I was new to the organization most of the conversations were on going. In other words, the things that were discussed were good information for me to know but I could not have any valid say so in most topics because I wasn't too knowledgeable of the topics that were being discussed. These meetings as well typically lasted 3-4 hours or more, on any given night during the week or weekend. What also made this process a little more difficult was that the graduate chapter was about a year or two old so they still were fairly new.

The President's meetings were held once or twice a month. These meetings typically were during the week and lasted between an hour or two. For a while the President's meetings and NPHC meetings were on the same night during the week, so for me those nights were pretty long. And the NPHC meetings would range from 1-2 hours depending on the topics being discussed. In addition to these meetings, I had to meet one on one with the NPHC advisor who sat down with me to discuss any progress, issues or concerns that I had with the organization or NPHC . These meetings typically lasted about 30 minutes which was just enough time for me to squeeze it in between classes and meetings. So as you can see, my calendar was pretty full. Between sorority and university meetings along with work and school, I was one busy bee. When I was dealing with these things, it didn't seem like this much until it slowly started to wear on my mind and body.

Like a Dripping Faucet, it Slowly Drained Me

What I explained above was more of a general outline of the types of things I would have to do being in the position that I was in. In this section, I briefly list the labor intensive work I did inside of the organization. I will expand briefly on each point. This list contains some of the things that others do not get to see unless they are on the other side of the organization.

- At times I had to drive 2 hours to another university to attend State Meetings and/or Retreats.
- There was meeting after meeting, some of which were required and those that were not required, attendance was strongly encouraged. Since I was part of a small chapter, if no one was available I was the one who went to these meetings.
- I had no time for myself. It was the sorority and school with a repeat of that each week.
- Having to juggle three separate calendars (sorority, NPHC, chapter) and have all of that information up to date in order and ready for the rest of the chapter to be informed and fulfill the duties in their roles was a full time job in itself. I definitely honed my organizational skills. There were thousands of dollars that were invested in the chapter and sorority as a whole from all the chapter members combined.
- There was a constant reminder to always get ready to bring in new members. Every time we tried to do just that something came up, or our grades went down, or we had to wait on Nationals.

At a glance, this list may not seem like anything out of the ordinary. But imagine if one didn't have all of the resources to execute this list, and imagine that this is your first time ever being in a position of leadership to this capacity. Better yet imagine you just starting up a chapter from the ground up with high expectations coming from everyone including yourself. In this instance one would have to hit the ground sprinting.

Stepping Down with Both Feet Out

When someone first joins a sorority, they stress over and over again that this is a lifetime commitment. In other words, they don't even want members to think of getting out because that means their secrets will be getting out too. With this in mind, and after two years with the sorority, I was beginning to feel boxed in. The relationship and the morals and values of the sorority were not giving me anything in return. It was just taking and I wanted out. This was not a reciprocating agreement between me and the sorority, and I was beginning to feel the burden of it. At this point, I have had it with frustrations and lack of seeing progress to any measurable amount, sizable enough for me to see, or even imagine. I was mentally and physically exhausted.

There were times when I was so stressed out that whenever someone would mention the name of the sorority, I would immediately stress out and be unhappy. I didn't want to wear the letters anymore, I wasn't proud to be a member of the sorority because I felt like I was a slave worker for the organization. I remember walking around campus and watching "normal" individuals happy and free. As I saw this I said to myself I wish I could be like them, I wish I was free. Little did I know my spirit was crying for help on the inside.

I wanted out. In this next section, I want to back up for a moment and describe the meeting that I had with some of the members, and how this was the first step in the process of me restoring my freedom again.

The Meeting: Decisions Decisions

After over a year of dissatisfaction and discontent from what has happened in the sorority so far, I was in desperate need of help, a remedy, and a sane mind. One evening, the chapter and I went to our chapter meeting at our State advisor's home. It was during this meeting that I decided to bring up the issues that I was dealing with and ask for some help. At this meeting, were the members of the undergraduate chapter I was a member of, the State Advisor and Undergraduate Advisor who phoned in to the meeting.

We were asked as a whole and individually how things were going and to share any concerns that we might have had. When it came to my turn, I spoke and stated in a nutshell that between my course load, FSP demands and sorority demands it was beginning to be too much. They asked me to give examples of what was too much. So, I told them that the emails and some other tasks were just beginning to be too much. Now, from the surface it seems remedial and not too hard of a task, and it isn't. I just was bogged down with so much that saying emails were too much was all I could get out. I just wanted some type of relief and emails would have done some of that. Now, when I expressed to everyone in the meeting that things were beginning to be too much and I needed a break, the response I got was laughter. The State Advisor laughed as if to mock at my misery and said that that's what they all had to do at our level and if

I think the duties of being president is too much then I should just step down. She basically told me oh well welcome to sisterhood.

Immediately getting teary eyed, the Undergraduate Advisor asked if I was OK...I said yes but I wasn't. I was angry, tired, stressed and was in need of a serious break. Mind you at the beginning we all committed to be in our positions for two years and for most in any sorority or fraternity, that is a long time and I see why. Every time I wanted to do something that was best for me, it seemed like I never could fully do that. I was always reminded of the commitment that I made to the organization and that it's not just about me. After her response, it was the last straw for me. I had to make some decisions.

The meeting proceeded and we finished up taking care of chapter matters. On the drive home, I had a talk with my line sisters and told them that I was seriously thinking of stepping down. They all said that they supported whatever decision I had to do but they strongly encouraged me to stay in the position because if I stepped down they knew what amount work was ahead and so did I. I was doing the bulk of things and as president there are a lot of decisions and emails that the other members don't see. They offered to help but nothing seemed to be a good solution for the issue.

This meeting and conversation happened just before we went on to Christmas break. So, I knew I had this time to think things over and come up with an answer before the new semester began. After the meeting and conversation went nowhere, I came to the realization that I had to make some decisions on my own for the good of my health and academics. At the first chapter meeting of the year, I announced that I was stepping down from the position of being president. The irony of it was, it seemed like no one cared, and as soon as I made the decision to step down one of the graduate members really started to take time and invest in the undergraduate chapter even though things were still progressing at the same pace.

After I stepped down from being president, I was able to breathe again and begin to really focus on what was important, my education. Little did I know, this was just the beginning of a new chapter in my life with a little taste of making adult decisions for myself and not being a people pleaser.

Chapter 4:
The Fork in The Road

Even though I had my ups and downs with the organization, I made the commitment of sticking with it through it all. It wasn't until God's light shined on the situation, that I realized what I was involved in was not beneficial for the kingdom of God. After this revelation, the turmoil and stress seemed to make sense. In this chapter, I will be talking about the fork in the road and what path I decided to take, and how I came to this decision.

The Feelings

In my last semester of my junior year, I was beginning to really feel disconnected from the sorority. There were plenty of times where I felt burdened and felt like I was in bondage and was in desperate need of freedom. Prior to stepping down from the position of president, I felt these similar feelings but they were suppressed by the responsibility and obligations of the position. There were times when I would walk the campus and think to myself, I want to be just like them. Meaning I wanted to be free from the sorority life just like any non Greek member. When I first thought this, I was astonished at myself because I was thinking wow, how can a non-profit organization make me feel like I have no freedom?

There were moments where I did not want to wear my letters. I didn't want people to know I was in a sorority because I knew inquiring minds want to know more detail; and at this point, talking about it even in the most general way brought stress for me. Little did I know, my soul was crying for a way out. Having brushed off the thought, I thought nothing of it any longer. These feelings however, were just the tip of the iceberg.

The Two Validations

It was around my last semester of junior year that the questioning of my membership to this organization came up yet again. One day, I was sitting in my room and my roommate (who is a member of a sorority) came in and showed me a video that a Christian woman did who was a former member of a sorority. She was explaining how all of the divine 9 organizations do not line up with the word of God. As soon as I saw this, I was immediately on the defensive and said, "I don't know what they do in her organization but the sorority that I am in does not do those things." After watching about 15 minutes of the video, I stopped watching it. Then a little while later, I had a hunch in my spirit that said, you might want to check this issue out further. At the time I did not do research right away because it was the end of the semester and quite frankly, there isn't time to do much of anything except your final exams and papers.

Once school was out, I had more time to really think and be away from the stressful environment. My first summer read was a book titled, "The Truth Behind Hip Hop." In this book, the author talks about the origins of hip hop and all of the symbolic meanings that are within. There was one section in the book that started to briefly speak about secret societies, fraternities and sororities…in the same sentence! This for me, was the last straw. I thought to myself, if fraternities and sororities can be categorized in the same area as secret societies, I knew that this is something I did not want to be a part of.

What I had been feeling about the organization was beginning to be validated. When I read this information, I began to pray to my Heavenly Father about it, and His response to me brought me to the fork in the road. He said to me in more ways than one that I was either going to choose Him or the sorority, I couldn't serve both. This was the moment I chose to live, serve and glorify the One and only Jesus Christ. Period. Once I knew that the Lord supported me I took on His confidence, strength and boldness and got out. No more lifetime commitment for me. The only life commitments I will ever have is marriage, and a relationship with God and that lasts through eternity! Truly, Jesus Christ is all I need.

Part II:
My Testimony.
Thank you Jesus Christ.

Chapter 5:
The Research

After I denounced all affiliation with the organization, I had a deep yearning to do a lot of research. The research is mainly about the origins of the organization and more importantly what God says about it in His word (the Bible). All summer before school I was in hibernation so to speak, with God's word and my computer. I have done research and read articles, videos, and books from those who oppose and promote Greek Lettered Organizations. The research that I did after I got out of the sorority should have been the type of research I was doing before I decided to get into a sorority. This type of research is precisely the reason why I have been led to write this book. People, Christians especially, have to be properly informed about everything. As a Christian, it is important to look at things from God's perspective, especially with something that is a lifetime commitment. There should be no surprises after you have signed on the dotted line.

God's Word is forever pregnant with new revelation. This tell us that we as humans do not know everything on our own. God tells us to study His word so that we can show ourselves approved (II

Timothy 2:15), so when something does not line up with the word of God, it becomes more apparent that something is not of God. In the following chapters, I am going to share my testimony and I hope you as the reader will either solidify or change your perspective on Greek Lettered Organizations and their role in your life.

Internet Research

As a starting point for my research, I immediately went to my computer and pulled up my favorite search engine: Google. My main focus of research is on Black Greek Lettered Organizations (BGLO). During my research I began looking up testimonies of others who have denounced their sorority or fraternity. I watched a few videos on YouTube that gave the audience a warning message about joining or continuing membership in a BGLO. When I watched these videos, I became inspired, and received confirmation that I too can help keep Christians informed about the truth of what's going on in Greek Life.

One thing I began to notice was that no matter what organization these members came from, they all were saying the same thing and shared similar concerns about things such as oaths, Greek gods and goddesses on a BGLO symbol and rituals. There are always activities that cause one to raise an eyebrow. For example, why is it that one can't drop the cane, or sit on the letters? Why is it that a cane and the Greek alphabet hold such sacred values?

One way I began doing research was by researching the origins of certain words and why they were used in a BGLO. For example, I looked up words such as, archon, which means: ruler or lord, or as a title of a specific public office. The office was usually one that rules over the civic, military, and religious affairs of the state.

It is very interesting that one organization has a group called the archonettes, even the magazine is called the Archon. The word archon can even be traced back to the early years of Gnosticism, which in that context referred to a servant of the "creator god" whose is named Demiurge.

Another example, the word Boule means a council of citizens appointed to run daily affairs of the city. A Boule in the GLO world is a Conference where all of the members come together and have various meetings and workshops about sorority or fraternity business. Other organizations call it a Conclave which literally means locked in. A Conclave is another term that can be found when talking about the pope and Vatican. Whenever the occasion arises for a new pope to come into office, there is a conclave (meeting) that is held to decide on who will arise to the position. Some of these points I am using may seem innocent or irrelevant, but everything has a meaning and purpose.

This area of research that I did was to help me understand the roots of certain words and how the remnants of ancient behavior are still present in the 21st century. There are tons and tons of history out there, much of which in order to speak about I would have to write a separate book about, but I just wanted to give you a glimpse of how you can begin your research if you are considering joining one, or are considering getting out of one. It is worth it to invest some time to do some research.

Freemason and Fraternity Connection

With this topic I started looking up information regarding the connection between black sororities and fraternities and freemasonry. I wanted to research this because freemasonry too is a secret society and I wanted to investigate more on the similarities between these two entities.

Whenever I would get Greek paraphernalia online, I always wondered why some websites would sell Greek paraphernalia along with freemasonry/order of the eastern star paraphernalia. My interest was piqued, so I started to dig beyond the surface. I think it is very interesting as to how many similarities can be found between the two.

Similarities

There are several similarities with freemason groups and Greek Lettered Organizations as a whole. I will supply a handful of examples in this category. To start we can talk about the rituals. In BGLO's there are usually one or two rituals that are traditionally used to initiate new members into the organization. Keep in mind that each organization is different, so the activities and knowledge specific to the organization will be different. During these rituals it is required that all new aspiring members wear all white garments. This is the same for new members in freemasonry. The purpose of wearing white is symbolic for being ready to receive a new identity with new knowledge.

In BGLO's there are oaths that each initiate takes, pledging their commitment to the organization. Also, there are hand grips that are only known by its members to confirm one's actual membership to the organization. These two practices can both be found in the practices and rituals of Freemasonry.

Both entities have initiates go through an initiation process that proves that they can be trusted and are worthy of wearing and representing the organization. Through these processes, an initiate is tested beyond their limits and must prove they will not "break" but keep going and persevere for the organization and its members. Both entities have pillars or principles that they stand on and that the organization is built upon. For example, the pillars of freemasonry are wisdom, strength and beauty. Many BGLO's will have scholarship and community service as their pillars as well.

Similar to free masonry, BGLO's do not release all information about the organization up front. In an informational meeting a person will gain the basic and minimal information that can be found anywhere even on an organization's website. Both freemasons and BGLO's are huge on humanitarianism and volunteerism. Both entities take credit for making a huge impact in America. For example, BGLO's are accredited for helping in advancing education within the African American community, as well as giving back to their community. Freemasons take credit for being some of the first responders to helping out the less fortunate or those in need after a disaster has hit.

Both entities have a vast networking system for its members, hence one of the reasons for the brotherhood and sisterhood aspect of the organizations. The last similarity that I am going to mention is that Freemasonry and BGLO's require that its members make a commitment to the organization for life. Keep in mind that one is asked to make a lifetime commitment without the full scope of what it takes to obtain and sustain membership. The conception of fear is birthed the moment someone signs and says yes to something they have no clue as to what is about to take place.

The research that I have shared with you was solely from books, prior knowledge, Wikipedia (as a start) and Google research. I want you as the reader to have a perspective from the information that's already out there combined with the experiences and knowledge I have based on being a former member of a Black Greek Lettered Organization. In the next chapter, I want to bring another perspective to the table; that is God's perspective from His Word, the Bible.

Chapter 6:
Studying the Word of God

As a Christian, it is important that we know what God says about everything. We have to constantly put His will before our own and trust that God knows what is good for us. When I officially denounced from the sorority, I began to really dig into God's Word to find out what He said about secret societies. In order to do this, I had to break the Word down even further and look for scriptures that talk about some of the things that fraternities and sororities do. For example, I began to do research on the topics of rituals, oaths, lies, freedom, bondage, etc.

I dug even further in the research of God's Word and began to parallel God's Word with the fraternity and sorority groups to see how one mirrors the other in an opposite way. In this chapter, I will break down some of the topics I researched, and explain what God says about it by quoting scripture. I will be showing you things from a spiritual perspective, how God sees things, and not from a worldly or carnal perspective.

Serving Two Masters

Jesus Christ said, "No one can serve two masters; for either he will hate the one and love the other, or else he will be loyal to the one and despise the other. You cannot serve God and mammon" –Matthew 7:16. Including myself, during the time I was in the sorority, I didn't think that being a part of a sorority meant I was serving a master. As far as I was concerned, I only served Jesus Christ, my Lord and Savior, no one else. However, as the Holy Spirit revealed to me a little deeper meaning concerning this topic, I realized that I indeed hated the sorority and loved God.

When I was in the sorority, I was unhappy and seemed to be working more on the sorority things more than anything else. Most of my time, money, efforts and creativity were going to help advance the sorority and not the kingdom of God. Now, from a carnal perspective, it may seem like GLO members may simply be multitasking the affairs of college life and work; but on a spiritual level, oh how the truth of God's word sheds light on the darkness!

Another indicator of how being an active member of the sorority/fraternity is like serving another god, is that a person feels condemnation. Why would someone feel condemnation from a sorority or fraternity? If I decided I did not want to participate in a step show, or go to a meeting because I wanted to focus on school, I should not be feeling condemn. In a "sisterhood" I thought love and support would come before condemnation. By the way, God never condemns His children; He only convicts them of their righteousness in Christ Jesus.

God says, "But that prophet or that dreamer of dreams shall be put to death, because he has spoken in order to turn you away from the Lord your God, who brought you out of the land of Egypt and redeemed you from the house of bondage, to entice you from the way in which the Lord God commanded you to walk..If your brother, the son of your mother, your son or your daughter, the wife of your bosom, or your friend who is as your own soul, secretly entices you, saying 'Let us go and serve other gods' which you have not known...you shall not consent to him or listen to him, nor shall you spare him or conceal him" –Deuteronomy 13:5-8.

The message from this scripture is that we are supposed to take caution to those who try to entice us to do things that are not of God and turn away from them in love.

Parallels

There are SEVERAL parallels that show not only how sororities and fraternities can be someone's master if they are a member, but also where someone's commitment and service is. The fact that I can parallel a non-profit organization to Christianity is very alarming, and lets people know that there is something more to it than just education and community service. Let's begin with the topic of money. As Christians, we are to give 10% of our income to God as tithe. The tithe is God's money which represents our willing heart to give God 10% and God's loving heart to let us keep 90%.

In Malachi 3:10, God says, "bring all of your tithes into the storehouse, that there may be food in My house, And try me now in this, says the Lord of hosts, if I will not pour out for you such blessing, there will not be room enough to receive it".

In this scripture God is saying, if we give Him 10% of the first fruits of our income, He will turn that around and bless us so much that we will not have room enough to receive it. That is very promising and exciting! Not only do we give 10% but we also give to those who are in need and to the church so that it can continue spreading the gospel through our offerings. As a Christian, we do these things because we love God and we know that He has our best interest in mind. Therefore, we are obedient to His Word.

Now, let's examine this same topic of money in terms of GLO's. In GLO's, they ask you for dues. I know for the sorority I was in, there were chapter, state and national dues that needed to be paid annually. All of which came up to be hundreds of dollars in a year, and thousands of dollars if you combine all of the members, plus dues that were owed to the university. Imagine, just imagine, if that money went to the kingdom of God to help spread the Gospel.

Spiritually speaking, those dues are like tithing to the GLO. All of one's money, resources and fundraising ideas all go towards advancing the sorority or fraternity, and not the kingdom of God. In exchange, one gets a lifetime of connections, a new family and everything they may need. But as you can see, the GLO becomes the provider and not God, who supplies all of our needs according to His riches in glory by Christ Jesus (Philippians 4:19).

I know some members of GLO's say they tithe to God and pay their dues to their organization without a problem. I did too. The problem is, that member is still serving two masters. With my experience, I was asked by God to choose whom I was going to serve, and of course I chose to serve Jesus Christ whole-heartedly. It takes money to advance any kingdom. What a person chooses to invest in, speaks and shows a lot.

Another area to parallel is the entire initiation process to become a member of a BGLO. To become a child of God one has to, "confess with their mouth the Lord Jesus Christ, and believe in their heart that God raised Him from the dead, they will be saved" –Romans 10:9. Once this happens, in the spiritual realm that person is a new man or woman. They no longer serve the world but God and will be going to heaven. One is now a part of the family of God and has all the rights and authority as a child of God in Christ Jesus.

The Holy Spirit now lives and dwells in the heart of a saved individual. Jesus Christ now abides in a child of God as they abide in Him, thus making them joined together as one. A new life, new identity in Christ Jesus, where the old things are put away and the new things are present. We now have purpose and begin to pursue the kingdom of God and His mission! Where we His children are the apple of His eye, and are protected by the King of kings, Jesus Christ. As a Christian we are now out from under the yolk of bondage and now freely walk in the freedoms that God has given us as His children, to be able to have a relationship with Him and know Him on a more intimate and personal level.

Once a person becomes a new initiated member of a BGLO, the members have now put away their old, individual selves and have been brought into the light of that particular organization as being one with their organization. New members now have a new history, new name, new identity, are identified by color and signs. A new family, new purpose, new mission, new attitude, and a wealth of resources and network of people are given to them. Those members now rely heavily upon the organization for a lot of things and some will go to the limits to protect their new identity (aka Greek letters). Now, new members are exposed to a little bit more of the things that go on in the organization that are exclusive only to its members. Can you see how BGLO's are set up for its members to serve them and allow it to consume their lives?

Another parallel are the "calls" that BGLO's do. There is a term called "role call," and this is where organizations say a chant or make a sound that is distinct and specific to their organization. Role calls are usually done at Greek social and business events. The call can also be served as a tool to help members find one another. So, if a member of an organization does their call, the other member will respond back to let them know that they are near. I wonder if members of BGLO's ever thought about who or what they are calling and channeling when they do those calls and chants. I know of an organization that can't say their calls under a roof, I think they believe it is bad luck.

As Christians, we do not chant or do calls. Rather we cry out to our Heavenly Father, give Him thanks, glory and praise through songs and hymns. We sing songs to the Lord to usher in His presence and be with Him in that moment. God says to love Him with all of your heart, and not lean on your own understanding and in all your ways acknowledge Him (Luke 10:27, Proverbs 3:5-6). When a Christian is a part of a GLO, do you think all of the things they do are acknowledging the Almighty God? How can one call on the Lord and to their organization at the same time...that just doesn't make any sense.

Another parallel is the armor of God. As a Christian, God tells us to put on His armor, which is the sword of the Holy Spirit, shield of faith, helmet of salvation, the breastplate of righteousness, girding the waist with truth, and shod your feet with the preparation of the gospel of peace (Ephesians 6:11-17). God tells us the reason for putting on His armor is because we are in a spiritual warfare and what we wrestle against are principalities, powers, rulers of the darkness of this age, and against spiritual hosts of wickedness in the heavenly places (Ephesians 6:12).

So when we talk about shields and preparing for battle it would be safe to say that both sides have their separate armor. Now, those who are initiated in a GLO have a new shield, and new symbols that represent different things. Could it be that the reason why new initiates have to wear all white is because they are preparing for their new identity, new life and new shield? Think spiritual here. Chew on it, and let it digest.

Rituals

One of the most alarming signs during the initiation process is going through rituals. I knew right away that being a part of two rituals was very suspicious, but because my mindset was fear, I didn't think too much further than that. As a Christian, we do not go through any rituals in order to become a child of God. We just simply believe and receive. I believe rituals represents symbolism in a sense that external rituals signify the mental and spiritual change that is occurring on the inside.

A ritual is another word or term for a type of pass over from one side to another. Spiritually, there is a transfer that is occurring and we have to ask ourselves, what are we saying, and why are rituals needed to be done if this is a Christian based organization? If someone is already a Christian, why is there a need to conduct rituals to do community service, and have relationships when this is something God called us to do anyway? These are just some things to think about. Rituals are religious and have no place in a Christian based organization.

Common Symbolism

There are many pieces or symbols that Greek Lettered Organizations use that are similar to Christianity. Those symbols that are used do not have Christian meaning. When most people see these symbols they automatically find a commonality between the Christian faith and the organization and therefore think it is ok to be a part of it without looking further into the way these symbols are used. The symbols have to line up with the actions. Words need corresponding action to confirm and verify the truth of what has been said and believed.

An example of common symbolism between the two entities is education and community service. In the GLO's some of the main pillars are education and community service. Actually, in order to become a member of a sorority or fraternity one has to be a student at a university or college and preferably already be doing community service in some capacity. It is safe to say that a member who has a good education is a valuable asset to the organization, has the capability to think creatively and help the organization grow.

Community service is an avenue in which the organization's name can get out there in the community and be known for helping out on a local and global level. As a Christian community service is done not only to help others, but also to help spread the Gospel and Good News of Jesus Christ. Both entities are doing the same wonderful things. The differences are, the credit is either going to

God or the GLO, and either one is getting an education and doing community service for the advancement of God's kingdom or the organization. Let me say, there is absolutely nothing wrong with doing community service or getting an education. However, it is very important that those two factors are not the sole reason why one decides to join a GLO.

Another common symbolism that one may see is the dove. The dove can be found in the shield of Zeta Phi Beta Sorority, Inc, and Phi Beta Sigma Fraternity, Inc. In Christianity, the dove represents the Holy Spirit. Semiramis, the queen of Babylon supposedly conceived a son named Nimrod while being a virgin. Semiramis is also represented as a dove. Now, as a Christian we know that Mary is the only woman who gave a virgin birth to her Son, Jesus Christ (Matthew 1:18, 23). Now what does that dove in the shield represent again? Do we really know which one it is? These are things I suggest you as the reader, conduct research on. There is a spiritual warfare going on and there are only two sides. We all must pick one side.

Scripture References According to Topic

People ask more times than one, "where is it in the Bible"? Well, I am here to tell you exactly what God says about common topics that come up when talking about Black Greek Lettered Organizations and what God says about some of the activities that are done. Below is a list of scriptures separated according to topic. I encourage you to take some time out and read them for yourself. Not only will it benefit you, but it will help you focus on what God says and not what someone said that God says. Each scripture shown below is separated by book, chapter and verse(s). For example, you would read Genesis 1:1 as, Genesis chapter one, verse one.

1. Bondage: Romans 6: 1-18, Galatians 5:1
2. Oaths: Matthew 5:33-37, James 5:12, Habakkuk 2:18-20, Hebrews 6: 12-18, Hebrews 7:28
3. Hazing: Romans 13:10
4. Worshipping False gods: Luke 16:13, Deuteronomy 13: 5-7
5. Fear: 2 Timothy 1:7
6. Deception/Secrecy: John 3: 18-21, Hosea 4:6
7. Unequally Yoked: 2 Corinthians 6:14-18
8. Spiritual Warfare: Ephesians 6:12, Galatians 5:1-25, 2 Corinthians 10: 3-6
9. Darkness: Ephesians 5: 6-17, John 3:21
10. Jesus Christ is the only Light: John 1:6-9, Romans 13:12-14. Be enlightened only by the word of God.

Chapter 7:
Advice for College Students

Advice is something that is invaluable when it comes to making important decisions in one's life. When I was deciding on whether or not I should join a sorority, I wish I had more people speak up around me and share their wisdom and insight on this issue. So, in return I will give a few pieces of advice for those college students who are interested in joining Greek Lettered Organizations. My first piece of advice to you is to DO YOUR RESEARCH. I cannot stress to you how important it is to not only look at each sorority or fraternity closely, but to weigh everything against your values and morals. Hopefully you will begin to see the organizations for what they are and make an informed decision at that time.

If you are not a Christian, I hope that you too will see that God isn't out to hurt you or take away your fun, but rather provide protection for you through His Son, Jesus Christ. Joining a fraternity or sorority is a big decision for any individual and it shouldn't be taken lightly. My prayer today is that you become saved and become secure and welcomed into the family of God through Jesus Christ. If you are a Christian, I advise you to get involved with a Holy Spirit led church. Create some friends and mentors who are focused on the Lord and are actively doing the will of God. Together as Christians, we can help and encourage each other along our walk with Christ. Now that is true brotherhood, the brotherhood of Christ.

Everyone is looking for that ultimate college experience they can share with others once they graduate, even if it is at a small price. The ultimate college experience is unique to the individual and can only be created once. College is what a person puts into it academically, and socially. If someone decides to study abroad for two semesters, or start up their own club on campus, it is up to them to make the most out of it and add it to their story of the ultimate college experience. There is more to college than the traditional pathways that have already been treaded on. Find your own unique way of enjoying college as a free individual. Take your time in making a decision or commitment, there is no rush.

Below are some key questions you should ask yourself when considering on whether or not joining a Greek lettered Organization is best for you:

1. Why do you want to join a Greek Lettered Organization?
2. What is it that intrigues you about a Greek Lettered Organization?
3. If you are a Christian, what actions or deeds of the Greek Lettered Organization have led you to want to be a part of the group?
4. What concerns or reservations do you have as you are learning more about Greek Lettered Organizations and their purpose?

5. What does God say about this in His word?

6. Are you considering joining an organization to please God and to advance His kingdom, or for selfish reasons?

7. Are you satisfied with making a lifetime commitment to an organization you don't know too much about initially?

Chapter 8:
Advice for Current Members
of a Greek Lettered Organization

I know what it's like to commit to a GLO for a lifetime and later on down the line realize that this is something that you don't want to do any more. I understand the feeling of thinking you've made a huge wrong turn, but are stuck and have no way out because of the lifetime commitment that you've made. Well, I am here to tell you that there is a way out, and that is through Jesus Christ. When I decided to get out of the sorority I was a part of, I fully operated in the Lord's strength, courage and most importantly, I trusted the Lord that everything would be OK. I was completely finished with the sorority and was ready to completely leave it behind. It was at that moment where God was able to move in my life and begin the mending process.

When I decided to leave and denounce the sorority, I was not prepared to lose some of the friendships that I had gained. My advice to anyone who is thinking of leaving their sorority or fraternity is to be prepared for some friendship loss, connections gone and being able to deal with emotions that one may feel. Know that God is with you and that the journey and purpose He has for you is much bigger and requires you to be free, so that His will be done and not our own. I don't think anyone is a bad person just because they are in a GLO. However, I do believe that as a Christian, one is either doing the works of God and pleasing the Lord, or one is doing the works of Satan. There is no lukewarm middle. God accepts us as we are and continues to work with us so that we can become the woman or man of God He has called us to be.

I have been through each and every stage, the beginning, middle and end of the "Greek experience". I am not perfect and have never been; I just love the Lord more than the opinion of others. I love everyone, Christian or non Christian very much. I encourage everyone to really put God first and step out on faith and seek God's counsel on whether or not being in a Greek Lettered Organization is pleasing in His sight. Most people don't have the courage to break away from their sorority or fraternity, but I tell you today that in the Lord's strength any and everything can be accomplished.

Below are some questions that I asked myself during my time as a member and after I denounced. I encourage you to ask yourself these same questions honestly.

1. How much desire did I have for God when I was in the sorority?
2. When I was a member of the sorority, how many people did I lead to Christ and how many to the organization?
3. What was I perpetuating? Why did people want so badly what I had as a result of being in a sorority?
4. How much research did I really do before I joined?
5. How much of my decision to join a sorority was solely my

decision and not the influence of the sorority or others' opinions?

6. Why is it that I felt more fear in the initiation process than faith in God?

7. I asked God to help me get through the initiation process, but I didn't ask specifically if I should even be enduring this process unnecessarily.

8. What do I have to gain from leaving the organization?

9. Who do you give thanks to first, God or your organization and its members?

Chapter 9:
Interviews

This section contains a handful of interviews, or perspectives, from current members of Greek Lettered Organizations and interested members at one point in time. When making an important and sound decision everyone needs to have all sides accessible. These interviews help you as the reader see insight from all angles and what others have gone through and their thought process on the subject of joining or leaving a Black Greek Lettered Organization. I do want to note that these responses are the sole opinions and thoughts of the interviewees. My opinions and thoughts are not mixed in to the responses.

Perspective #1

1. Are you a Christian?

   - Yes.

2. Are you a part of Black Greek Lettered Organization? If so, which one?

   - Yes I am, but only on paper; my heart isn't.

3. Have you ever denounced a BGLO?
   - **No.**

4. Did you complete the initiation process?
   - **Yes. I wanted to drop but when I literally cried and told them of my intentions to do so, they acted like they cared about how I was feeling and really wanted me to continue, so I did. Since I had friendship ties with them prior to initiation, I felt bad for wanting to drop so against my better judgment, I continued.**

5. After completing the initiation process how did it make you feel?
   - **I felt like I had no reason to want to be affiliated with neither the organization nor the members. I didn't feel excited that I was finally in and I couldn't understand why people would put their friends through that. I remember wishing I had done the "paper" process. At least I wouldn't have had any animosity towards them.**

   I'm sure it weakened our friendship in the end and it shook me emotionally. I felt that the "process" couldn't have been what the organization was built on because if so, it's bound for destruction; I don't think it would still be in existence. Some chapters handle their initiation processes differently. They all said it would be worth it in the end and everyone would move forward and be so happy to be in the sorority, but I didn't and it wasn't worth the time or effort; I felt I had lost more than I had gained. The gifts they gave me just made it worse and

for several reasons, some of which I'm still unsure of, I didn't want to accept them.

6. Why did you want to join a Greek Lettered Organization?

   - I joined to find community, to connect with more African American students, and because it seemed like such a big deal for African American students to join a BGLO. I didn't like the university I attended because I felt I didn't fit in and I had trouble making real friends who I could relate to, or even just talk to. Then I went to NPHC's Meet the Greeks event, and it seemed great that (mostly) African American students came together to do community service, develop leadership and organizational skills, build life-long bonds, and be there for one another. I was on the verge of transferring but I thought if I joined an organization I would meet people who had common interests and I wouldn't feel so isolated from people. I thought it would have provided me with the missing piece that would enhance my undergraduate experience. Unfortunately, if didn't work out the way I expected and at times I feel even more lonely and isolated than before I joined.

7. What is one pro and one con from being in a GLO?

   -Pro-it can be a great networking opportunity to connect with people in another city, another state, or even another country so there will always be a group of people to call on and even trust while in an unfamiliar area.

-Con- Although they emphasize "prioritize" in words, many times it is expected that members put the organization first, before school and before actual family; they don't seem to fully understand that there is life outside and beyond the organization.

8. What kind of research did you do when you considered joining a GLO?

-Not much, just enough to be able to decide which one I felt would suit me, more or less, the best. When people said "do research" I didn't know what to look for, they all seemed very similar in purpose. I didn't think I had to dig deep or try to find information that they may be hiding. It seemed unnecessary since at the time, I didn't know anyone who had anything negative to say about **NPHC**. I read their national sites, some chapter websites, went to as many on-campus events and informational as possible, and I talked to my God sister who was attending an **HBCU**.

9. At the time, what were your views on secret societies (if any)?

-I didn't really have an opinion about secret societies since I didn't know about them; I didn't consider **NPHC** organizations as secret societies because I thought, if they were really secret I wouldn't know about them at all. It didn't really hit me until I had a conversation with students from other universities during a summer program. I met a girl who is Christian and opposes sororities and she explained why. She said it is mainly because they went against the Bible and were so secretive; but she didn't have the scriptures to prove it. Although I thought she was taking it too seriously and couldn't see anything good about it, she made me start thinking about what I was about to get myself into. I still thought it was something positive: they gave scholarships, did community service, were a presence in the community, and seemed to be more or less professional about their business and events. I just didn't like drama and when people tried to fight when their organization was "disrespected" or became really upset if their organization was made fun of. It all seemed immature. In the end, I brushed it off and proceeded.

10. Have you ever had thoughts of leaving your lifetime commitment to your organization? If so, why?

-I plan to leave my organization before the end of the year because it has caused me undue stress and I'm not in a comfortable place within myself. I told some of the members I don't think I will be in the organization forever because it's just not what I expected and I'm not happy. I don't look forward to doing things with the organization. I'm not going to participate in the initiation of new members and I will not accept the twisted, misled, ignorant belief that hazing is an acceptable tradition as long as nobody gets killed. It's not ok; it's not the way to build anything life-long.

Thinking about it irritates me because I can't believe I went through with it.

It's almost like reliving the experience. I could never yell at my friends who are being initiated in an organization I claimed to love and wanted them to be a part of. That's illogical. They didn't have to do things the way they did, they could have carried out initiation anyway they wanted to.

11. Would you recommend Greek Life to anyone?

-I would just tell people what to look for, what to look out for. I would tell people to make sure they know what they're getting into and make sure they understand and are firm in their own beliefs of what is ok and what isn't and encourage them to listen to themselves because in the end it all falls on them. People will hear what they want to hear, not necessarily what was said. I would tell them to just make sure it's something they want to do.

12. As a Christian, do you believe all activities of BGLO's line up with the word of God?

- On paper, yes. They claim to want to improve the community, educate, mentor, instill positive characteristics, and be role models. However, the practices are not always in line. There are some people who do their best to stay in line with the word of God and I have met some great people who are in an NPHC organization but they are individuals and they are often overshadowed and overpowered by their chapter.

In addition, when some people know about "illegal activity" taking place, instead of reporting it or confronting the chapter and threatening to report them, they just make sure they aren't caught in the mix. It's not right; it's our duty especially as Christians, to look out for the well-being of others.

13. Is there anything else that you would like to share?

- I've seen the good and the bad. Some people change themselves for the better to uphold the image of their organization and try to contribute to society through community service, mentoring and other forms of outreach. However, some people take it as an opportunity to manipulate others. I've had some of my prophytes, who also claim to be my friends, try to tell me what to do or make rude comments *after* I crossed just because I was a neophyte. They tried to make me do strolls when I didn't want to and get really upset about it, saying I'm not being "owt".

Where does it end? I told one of my close acquaintances, who is a member of another sorority, and she said they were mean and her chapter doesn't do that, at all. There's a negative culture associated with **NPHC** that is a minor contributor to the problem, especially for undergraduates.

People will ask me all sorts of questions that don't pertain to them, making assumptions and judgments. In addition, it's like being a celebrity, with all of the drama and rumors and comments and pictures and passed conversations, etc. Everyone believes once you're in, it's truly forever and there's no way out. But if there's a way in, there's a way out.

Perspective #2

1. Are you a Christian?

    - I am a new creature in Christ, so yes.

2. Are you a part of Black Greek Lettered Organization? If so, which one?

    - No. I only use Greek letters for calculus.

3. What kind of research did you do when you considered joining a GLO?

    - I asked current members and older alumnus of the organizations. I skimmed some Black Greek literature available at bookstores, and listened to sermons and websites that spoke about the topic of BGLO.

4. At the time, what were your views on secret societies (if any)?

    - I was captivated by the glamour and prestige of the BGLO. They were mostly leaders and well known on my campus.

5. Would you recommend Greek Life to anyone?

    - If you take you Christian walk seriously, then no.

6. As a Christian, do you believe all activities of BGLO's line up with the word of God?

- No, I do not believe all activities line up. That is not to say that there aren't activities that they do are noteworthy however we must not be luke warm as Christians.

7. Is there anything else that you would like to share?

   - As Christians we have a standard to uphold and we should do all that we can to be a light to the World and please our Father in every deed. Condemnation can only come from the Father and fellow Christians must be conscience of their affiliations with the world.

Perspective #3

1. Are you a Christian?

   - Yes

2. Are you a part of Black Greek Lettered Organization? If so, which one?

   - Yes.

3. Have you ever denounced a BGLO?

   - No

4. Did you complete the initiation process?

   - Yes.

5. After completing the initiation process how did it make you feel?

   - The initiation process was 16 weeks from initial interest meeting to initiation. Each stage of the process was different and made me feel differently. Nervous, scared, insecure, happy, relieved, confused, angry, disappointed, proud, humble, invincible, are some of the feelings and emotions that I felt during the entire process.

6. Why did you want to join a Greek Lettered Organization?
   - I initially wanted to join a Greek Letter Organization because of the popularity. I specifically joined my fraternity because of their reputation and power.

7. What is one pro and one con from being in a GLO?
   - One pro of being in a GLO is the networking opportunities.
   - One con of being in a GLO is the financial commitment.

8. What kind of research did you do when you considered joining a GLO?
   - I spoke with Professors and friends.

9. At the time, what were your views on secret societies (if any)?
   - I had a positive opinion of Secret Societies. The Shriners and Shriners' Hospital paid the surgical expenses and physical therapy for my little sister and little brother so that they would be able to walk (both have Cerebral Palsy). Without their financial support, my siblings would have remained crippled.

10. Have you ever had thoughts of leaving your lifetime commitment to your organization? If so, why?

   - Yes. I have thought about leaving. I have been concerned about the violence, lack of leadership, lack of vision, and lack of accountability.

11. Would you recommend Greek Life to anyone?

   - I believe that some people can benefit from being a member of a "group". However, it is not for everyone. Each person has to decide what is best for them. I will only educate and inform. People must make their own choices.

12. As a Christian, do you believe all activities of BGLO's line up with the word of God?

   - No. There are several activities that GLO members engage in that do not line up with the word of God. However, I am not aware of any organization that 100% lines up with the word of God. If so, there would not be over 50,000 Christian denominations in the U.S.A. with over 50,000 interpretations of the word of God.

13. Is there anything else that you would like to share?

   - I do not believe that BGLO's should still exist. I think that they served a good purpose when they were originally founded, but that purpose no longer exists.

Chapter 10:
Beginning of a New Journey

It is such a personal decision to leave or join a sorority or fraternity. When I denounced from the sorority, I knew that there was going to be a huge shift in my personal and social life. The Lord prepared me for it for sure! The many 'friends' that I had disappeared, people began to treat me differently, and I had people I didn't even know dislike me because I wasn't a member of the sorority any more. Leaving the sorority allowed me to see who my real friends are, the ones who loved me regardless and supported me through the tough transition period. It was at this time I really leaned on the Lord for support and protection, and I trusted in the Lord 100% and allowed Him to direct me on the path that He has laid out for me. I was able to let go of my past in all areas of my life and rededicate my life to Jesus Christ. The peace of the Lord that I felt and still feel after leaving the sorority is a feeling I will always hold on to.

Since I have denounced from the sorority, my life has changed in many ways. Now, I am free to live the life God has called me to walk in, and truly keep Him first in everything that I do. My relationship with God continues to elevate to higher levels every day and the bond that I have with Jesus Christ is something I will never give up for anything or anyone. Life after the sorority is like starting over again. Now, I have the time and money to invest into the kingdom of God and share testimony after testimony so that others may become informed about the topic.

Many people ask if I miss being in a sorority and my answer is no. I have learned some valuable lessons from being in a sorority, good and bad, and that is all I have taken from the experience. I pray often for those that did the initiation process with me because I want them to understand and know where I am coming from and that one day they too may make the decision to dig deeper into the word of the living God. I am so blessed and thankful that God shielded me from having animosity and anger towards the sorority. He also shielded me from having doubts about my decision to leave. My God is good and nothing but good comes from Him.

I am now on a journey in Christ and my testimony is just the beginning not only for me, but also for those who read this book.

Glossary

BGLO- Black Greek Lettered Organizations

FSP- Fraternity and Sorority Programs

GLO- Greek Lettered Organization

Line- A line in a BGLO literally means that each initiate lines up in one line. This line has significance and meaning to those that are going through the process together.

NPHC- National Pan Hellenic Council

Probate- This is an event where the newest member have a show in front of friends, family and others to showcase the new person they have become. At a probate, most new members cite their history and give thanks to everyone involved in their process.

Bibliography

Lewis, G. Craige. *The Truth Behind Hip-Hop. (United States of America: Xulon Press: 2009).*

Johnstone, Michael. *The Freemasons*: The Illustrated Book of an ancient Brotherhood. (New York: Metro Books, 2005), 101, 109, 118.

The Holy Bible: New King James Version. Thomas Nelson, 1982.

Wikipedia. *Archon.* http://en.wikipedia.org/wiki/Archon

Wikipedia. *Boule: Ancient Greece.* http://en.wikipedia.org/wiki/Boule_%28ancient_Greece%29

Wikipedia. *Gnosticism.* http://en.wikipedia.org/wiki/Gnosticism